# 50 Things Every College Student Should Know

*Because the Most Important Lessons You Learn Happen Outside the Classroom*

ANTONIO NEVES

Copyright © 2016 Antonio Neves
All rights reserved.

ISBN: 1523954949
ISBN 13: 9781523954940
Library of Congress Control Number: 2016902627
CreateSpace Independent Publishing Platform
North Charleston, South Carolina

*It's your life, so you have the last word. Make it special.*

# TABLE OF CONTENTS

| | | |
|---|---|---|
| Introduction | | ix |
| 1 | Make a Choice | 1 |
| 2 | Would You Bet on You? | 2 |
| 3 | Listen More Than You Talk | 4 |
| 4 | Surround Yourself With Greatness | 6 |
| 5 | You Don't Climb a Mountain By Accident | 8 |
| 6 | If You're on Time, You're Late | 10 |
| 7 | Find the Edge | 11 |
| 8 | Don't Start Your Day With Social Media | 13 |
| 9 | From Good to Great | 15 |
| 10 | It Doesn't Matter What College You Attend | 16 |
| 11 | Focus on What You Can Control | 18 |
| 12 | Be the Only One | 19 |
| 13 | Take Action on Your Ideas | 21 |
| 14 | The Best Time to Build Your Brand Is Now | 22 |
| 15 | Turn Up the Volume | 24 |
| 16 | Supporters Are Greater Than Followers | 26 |
| 17 | Get Your Priorities Straight | 28 |
| 18 | Communicate Like a Pro | 29 |
| 19 | Use the Ingredients That You Have | 31 |
| 20 | Choose Excitement Over Fear | 33 |
| 21 | It's Not Who You Know. It's Who Knows You. | 34 |
| 22 | The "Hustle" Is Real | 35 |

| | | |
|---|---|---|
| 23 | Complaining Doesn't Help | 36 |
| 24 | Know What You're Feeling | 37 |
| 25 | Work in the Service Industry | 38 |
| 26 | What's Your Story? | 40 |
| 27 | Set Others Up for Success | 42 |
| 28 | Travel Far & Wide | 43 |
| 29 | Talk to Yourself More Than You Listen to Youself | 45 |
| 30 | Tattoos Are Permanent | 46 |
| 31 | The Most Powerful Meeting You Can Have | 48 |
| 32 | What to Do When You Don't Know What to Do | 50 |
| 33 | Just Because You're Good at Something… | 51 |
| 34 | Collaborate | 53 |
| 35 | Tell a Story, Not the Whole Story | 54 |
| 36 | Job Interviews: Have an Agenda | 55 |
| 37 | Four Questions to Ask When Things Go Bad (or Good*) | 57 |
| 38 | Find Good Friction | 58 |
| 39 | Say it Before You Run Out of Breath | 60 |
| 40 | Your Family & Friends Won't Always Understand | 61 |
| 41 | "Us" & "We" Is Greater Than "I" & "Me" | 63 |
| 42 | Avoid the Place You Go to Give Up | 64 |
| 43 | Write Handwritten Thank You Cards | 66 |
| 44 | Break the Cycle | 67 |
| 45 | Your First "Real Job" Won't Be Your Last Job | 68 |
| 46 | It's Just Water | 70 |
| 47 | Give Thanks, Then Give Back | 72 |
| 48 | There Are No Metrics for Grit & Resilience | 74 |
| 49 | No One Cares More Than You | 76 |
| 50 | Stay Curious | 77 |

| | |
|---|---|
| Finally, Have Fun | 79 |
| Acknowledgements | 80 |
| About the Author | 81 |

# INTRODUCTION

A Google search about me will tell you that I hold a master's degree from an Ivy League university. It will reveal that I worked in the television industry in New York City for over 10 years as a correspondent, reporter, and producer. You'll also find that I'm a nationally recognized leadership speaker who has delivered keynotes to thousands upon thousands of people. Sounds great, right?

Well, that's what Google tells you. But it turns out, it doesn't tell you the *whole* story.

What a Google search won't tell you is that I'm from a small town — the kind of small town that people don't end up leaving. It won't tell you that I grew up experiencing a lot of chaos and instability; that before I graduated from high school, I moved over 15 times. And it won't tell you that I was the first generation of my family to go to college. But this is a major part of the story.

Early on, I knew that attending and graduating from college was my opportunity to create a new path for myself and break the cycle. And I did.

College changed my life. I excelled in the classroom, competed as an NCAA student athlete, studied abroad, worked part-time jobs, interned at top companies, had my heart broken, and made friendships that have lasted to this day. Most importantly, it started my journey of learning that what made me different, if not an outsider at times, was something to celebrate – not hide.

Interestingly, the most powerful lessons that I learned during my college years didn't take place in the classroom. They all happened in the world outside of it. That's what this book is all about: Those simple yet critical lessons that will set you up for a bright future.

Life is about choices – the choices we do and do not make. So thank you for *choosing* to read this book. I expect great things from you and would love to hear about them.

Antonio Neves
an@theantonioneves.com
www.TheAntonioNeves.com
@TheAntonioNeves

# 1

## MAKE A CHOICE

**Every day, you have the opportunity to make a choice:** A choice to be exceptional, or a choice to be average.

You can't be both.

The exceptional are willing to do what others won't to succeed. The average follow the crowd and accept "good enough."

"Good enough" is not enough.

# 2

## WOULD YOU BET ON YOU?

**Imagine that you're in Las Vegas and you walk into a casino.**

You pass by people betting their money on slot machines, blackjack tables, and roulette wheels. Then you walk into the "sports book" area where people are betting on events like football, horse races, basketball, and baseball.

Something grabs your attention. Your name is on the big board. People are betting on you! They're betting on whether you will, or will not, accomplish your goals in life. Here's a question:

*Would you be willing to bet on you actually accomplishing all your goals and all those things you say are most important? Would you bet on you doing what it takes to make this happen?*

That's a big question. Now let's take it a step further.

*Would you be willing to let your family and friends spend their hard-earned money betting that you will accomplish all of your goals and all those things you say are most important? Would you allow them to bet on you doing what it takes to make this happen?*

For the odds-makers in Vegas, your odds of success are easy to determine. All they have to do is take a look at what you did yesterday, the day before that, last week, the month before, etc. Like a sports team, this is your record.

Until you're willing to bet on you, and do the hard work that's required, it's impossible to get others to do the same. How much you give or don't give is up to you.

So, would you be willing to bet on you doing what it takes to accomplish your most important goals in life? Would you bet on you following through and staying committed? Would you bet on you taking that first step today?

# 3

## LISTEN MORE THAN YOU TALK

**The most valuable thing you can give someone is your attention.**
It's no coincidence that you have two ears and one mouth. The universe got it right.

Good listeners don't think about what they're going to say next when the other person is speaking.

Good listeners ask follow-up questions.

Good listeners make it all about the person they're with — not about them.

So put your phone down.

Listen.

Ask questions.

Say, "Tell me more about that."

Be genuinely interested in someone's story.

When you do this, you earn trust and can truly connect with others.

Listen more than you talk. This is how you become the most interesting person in the room.

# 4

## SURROUND YOURSELF WITH GREATNESS

**You can spend time with *Thieves* or *Allies*.**
*Thieves* are those people who never encourage, support, or empower you. They don't challenge you. They don't inspire you. They don't hold you accountable. And they don't push you to be the absolute best version of yourself.

*Thieves* are energy vampires that zap all of your drive. *Thieves* always have drama going on. *Thieves* settle for mediocrity. *Thieves* can bring out the worst in you.

*Allies* are those people who always encourage, support, and empower you. They do challenge you. They do inspire you.

They do hold you accountable. And they do push you to be the absolute best version of yourself.

*Allies* give you energy. *Allies* always have great things going on in their lives. *Allies* won't accept anything but the best. *Allies* bring out the best in you.

Think about the five people you spend the most time with and ask yourself this question: **Do they make you better?**

Identify the *Thieves* in your life and create boundaries.

Find your *Allies* and keep them close. Be an ally to others.

Don't be afraid to work with the best. Surround yourself with greatness.

# 5

# YOU DON'T CLIMB A MOUNTAIN BY ACCIDENT

**Confidence is earned.**

If you were miraculously dropped off at the top of Mount Everest (a nearly 30,000-ft. altitude), what would happen? You would take in the view for a second and then you would pass out, or, maybe die.

Why? Because your lungs have not *earned* being at that high altitude.

This is the reason that the careers of reality stars tend not to last long. Two or three years after they win the big competition on television, they typically disappear.

Why? It's not necessarily that they're not talented or gifted. It's because they haven't done the necessary work to stay at the top of the mountain.

Before a comedian does the big television special, she has worked for years practicing her craft and performing at small comedy clubs. Before the band you love sells out a stadium, they have played at countless small venues getting their sound just right.

Confidence is earned.

Be willing to do the work and earn your way to the top of the mountain. This way you won't pass out, and can instead take in the amazing view.

# 6

## IF YOU'RE ON TIME, YOU'RE LATE

**Always show up early and plan ahead.**
"Traffic was bad" is not an acceptable excuse.

If you're on time, you're late.

# 7

## FIND THE EDGE

*"If you're not close enough to the edge, then you're taking up too much space."*
To grow, we have to be willing to get *uncomfortable*. The only way a muscle can grow bigger is by lifting heavy weights. When you lift heavy weights, your muscle actually tears. Then something miraculous happens – it grows back bigger and stronger.

*Finding the Edge* means being willing to regularly get uncomfortable.

If you've ever been an athlete before, you know that feeling you get before a game, match, or race begins when your heart starts racing and you get butterflies in your stomach. *That's Finding the Edge.*

If you've ever been a performer before, you know that feeling you get before you take the stage when your palms get sweaty or your throat starts to feel dry. *That's Finding the Edge.*

And if you've ever had a crush on someone, you know that moment when you finally ask them out on a date and you stutter your words while you feel like your heart's going to explode? *That's Finding the Edge.*

Think about the last week of your life. Now think about the last month. When was the last time you felt that increased heart rate? When is the last time you felt that nervous energy? When is the last time you felt butterflies in your stomach?

When is the last time you found the edge?

If you don't find the edge and regularly get uncomfortable, odds are you aren't growing, developing, and moving forward in life.

Push yourself. Find the Edge.

# 8

## DON'T START YOUR DAY WITH SOCIAL MEDIA

**Mornings are a powerful time.**
A time to set intentions. A time to get focused. And a time to see what we missed on social media. Right? Wrong!

Starting your day by checking social media is like being yelled at by thousands of people at the same time.

It might even cause you to feel like you're beginning your day by having to catch up with the rest of the world. This can cause you to feel anxious.

Instead, push pause and start your day off with purpose.

Set intentions. Identify what's most important. Be still.

Own your day, don't let it own you.

# 9

## FROM GOOD TO GREAT

**Remember: Good enough isn't enough.**
Never submit a major assignment, report, or project without first getting feedback from someone who can help make something better.

Sure, doing this can be vulnerable. And that's the point. This is where the magic happens and our biggest learning opportunities appear.

Be willing to take something from being good to great.

# 10

## IT DOESN'T MATTER WHAT COLLEGE YOU ATTEND

**Whether you attend an Ivy League university or a state school, it really doesn't matter.**
The college admissions process has been hijacked. It has become big business. "Best Colleges" lists don't tell the whole story. Instead, they make families and students seriously anxious. This is unnecessary.

What really matters is that you earn your degree, maintain a positive attitude, and work so hard and garner amazing experiences that it makes it impossible for people to ignore you. Do this regardless of what college is on your resume.

Believe it or not, the vast majority of successful people like CEOs, athletes, entrepreneurs, or executives didn't attend colleges at the top of the rankings. Many attended colleges and universities that you may have never heard of.

Regardless of what college or university that you attend, your job is to be so good that you can't be ignored. Use whatever college you attend to your advantage and be proud to get your education.

# 11

## FOCUS ON WHAT YOU CAN CONTROL

**There are things in our control and things outside of our control.**
You can't control the weather, but you can use an umbrella to stay dry in the rain.

Focus on what you can control.

Release what you can't.

# 12

## BE THE ONLY ONE

**It's easy to be part of the crowd and do what everyone else does.**
However, find time on and off campus to *be the only one*.

Find places to be the only person of your:

>Gender
>Ethnic Background
>Religion
>Nationality
>Political Party
>Etc.

When we experience being the only one, we learn to connect with others who have different viewpoints and backgrounds. We learn how much we may have in common with others. We learn to walk into any room and feel comfortable in our own skin.

Our differences can bring us closer.

# 13

## TAKE ACTION ON YOUR IDEAS

**Don't show up with just an idea.**
Prior to sharing and idea with someone, do as much research as possible, find successful examples in the marketplace, be prepared to answer any challenges, build a prototype, etc.

Make it easy for people to say yes.

# 14

## THE BEST TIME TO BUILD YOUR BRAND IS NOW

**Open up a private web browser and Google your name.** What do the search results show? Is it actually you? Is it someone who has the same name as you? Is it something that you posted on social media that you're embarrassed about?

The good news is that you can control search results by building a strong personal brand.

First, use a free web service like about.me to create a free personal website. Once you build it, use this link in your emails and social media profiles.

Next, go to a website like namecheap.com or register.com and buy your name (i.e., www.yourname.com). It should cost you less than $15.

Control what comes up when someone Googles you so you can be proud of what people find.

# 15

## TURN UP THE VOLUME

**When I worked as a local news reporter in New York City, I walked into my news director's office one day.** He was watching reels that reporters from across the country had mailed to him with the hopes of getting a job at the station.

I noticed that when he watched the reels, he viewed them with the television muted. He couldn't hear one word that the reporters were saying. I was confused.

So I asked him, "How do you know if you want to hire someone if you can't hear what they're saying?"

He looked at me, smiled, and said, "*I want to see if I want to turn up the volume.*"

Every day people are making a decision about whether or not they want to *"turn up the volume"* on you to support you and help you accomplish your goals.

They do this based on what time you arrive to class. They do this based on your attitude. They do this based on how you present yourself. They do this based on your resume. They do this based on your body language. They do this based on the questions you ask. They even do this when they Google your name.

Make great choices. This makes it easy for people to want to "turn up the volume" on you.

# 16

## SUPPORTERS ARE GREATER THAN FOLLOWERS

**Social media is awesome.**
It feels good to get that new follower, that like, that heart, the double-tap, the RT, that view, that subscriber, you name it.

Regardless how many "followers" you have, know this: *real life supporters are greater than social media followers.*

On those days when everything seems to be going wrong, real life supporters will be there for you to provide guidance and a pat on the back. Followers won't.

When things are going great, supporters will take you out celebrate. Followers won't.

Likes, RTs, hearts, double-taps, subscribers, views, and shares are great. However, they can never replace true human connection.

# 17

## GET YOUR PRIORITIES STRAIGHT

**As a college student, you have a lot of responsibilities.** To stay on top of things and not fall behind, it's critical to stay on top of your priorities.

Regularly ask yourself what's most important about today, this week, this month, this semester, etc.

Know what's important and what's not important. This allows you to focus.

You can do anything you want, but you can't do everything.

# 18

## COMMUNICATE LIKE A PRO

**Being able to communicate with confidence is a game-changer.**
It's the difference between getting people to believe in you or forget about you.

If your professors are inspired by your passion, they'll invest in you and your college experience.

If employers trust you, they'll hire you for that internship.

If fellow students believe you, they'll get behind your organization.

Many people struggle with interpersonal communication skills and feel painfully awkward. If this is you, don't stress.

The way to become a better communicator is to practice, practice, and you guessed it, practice.

# 19

## USE THE INGREDIENTS THAT YOU HAVE

**Great chefs are unique.**
If a chef wants to make a dish that requires ten ingredients, but they only have seven of the ingredients and no way of obtaining the other three, what will they do?

Are they going to complain, starve, or go to bed early that night? No.

A great chef will get excited and find a way to get creative with the 7 ingredients that they do have and make a delicious dish.

The greatest innovations tend to come under constraints. Use your disadvantages to your advantage.

You may not have the right amount of money in your bank account, but you can get a job.

You may not have access to a big network, but the staff and professors at your university do.

You may not have the right software on your computer, but there's a computer lab on your campus that does.

You may not live in the city where you want to live, but you can schedule a weekend to visit and get a feel for what it's like to live there.

Focus on the ingredients you have, not the ones you don't.

# 20

## CHOOSE EXCITEMENT OVER FEAR

**Fear and excitement are very similar emotions.**
The good news is that you get to choose which emotion you take on.

Next time you find yourself in fear about something, take a breath and ask, *"What excites me about this?"*

This small but important shift allows us to focus on the many opportunities instead of the few problems.

# 21

## IT'S NOT WHO YOU KNOW. IT'S WHO KNOWS YOU.

**We've always heard, "It's not what you know, it's *who* you know."**
This requires a minor, yet important tweak.

Actually, it's not who you know – it's who knows you.

You may be familiar with a lot of people, but if they're not familiar with you, your work, and your goals, who you know will do you no good.

Build strong relationships on and offline that create value for others.

# 22

## THE "HUSTLE" IS REAL

**The word "hustle" is all the rage.**
If you're hustling, allegedly, you're working hard to deliberately make things happen. And if that's the case, then great.

Just know that that people who are actually "hustling" aren't going to have time to tell you how hard they're hustling.

Why? Because they're too busy hustling.

# 23

## COMPLAINING DOESN'T HELP

**Complaining and blaming others is easy.**
The great don't do this.

Instead, those who succeed acknowledge what's going on around them and figure out how to make their situation better.

The great take full responsibility and accountability for their actions. They do what they say they're going to do. They keep agreements.

Most importantly, they ask themselves what they can *learn* from each situation.

# 24

## KNOW WHAT YOU'RE FEELING

**Sometimes when we're afraid, we're actually really excited.**

Sometimes when we're sad, were actually really angry.

Sometimes when we're angry, were actually really sad.

When you're feeling any type of emotion that may cause you to behave in a questionable manner, press pause and ask yourself, *"What am I really feeling?"*

When we ask ourselves this question, we create an opportunity to connect instead of disconnect.

# 25

## WORK IN THE SERVICE INDUSTRY

**Service industry jobs are one of the most powerful experiences that you can have in your life.**
Whether you work as a server at a restaurant, a front desk attendant at a hotel, or a salesperson at a retail store, this experience will provide you with a unique understanding of people.

You'll see the good, the bad, and the ugly. In the same day, you may get yelled at for something that wasn't your fault or rewarded with a large tip for awesome service.

What you'll walk away with is the ability to communicate with anyone, problem-solve on the fly, and learn how to become a creative thinker. These experiences also allow you to feel what it's really like to earn a paycheck so you never take it for granted.

Many people run away from service industry jobs. Think twice before you do. Though they may not be glamorous, service industry jobs set you up for life and career success.

# 26

## WHAT'S YOUR STORY?

**Over the course of your life, you're going to regularly get asked, "*What's your story?*" or "*Tell me about yourself.*"**
Don't let this question catch you off guard.

Most people give a chronological response to questions like these.

*"Well…I was raised in X town…I went to X college…I studied X… I work for X…I live in X…"*

These answers, well, they're boring.

Instead, get creative with your answer. Take time to identify a few things about you and your story that make you unique. These are those things that would never show up in a Google search or on your resume.

Your goal when you answer this question is for someone to respond, "Tell me more about that."

# 27

## SET OTHERS UP FOR SUCCESS

*"You can have everything in life you want, if you will just help enough other people get what they want."*

*-Zig Ziglar*

**When you help others shine, you shine.**
Be an ally to someone.

Set others up for success.

# 28

## TRAVEL FAR & WIDE

**Travel is life changing.**
A college career isn't complete without studying abroad. Sadly, only a small percentage of students make this choice.

A semester or year abroad will allow you to live in another country, study a foreign language, and give you a better understanding of other cultures, and most importantly, yourself.

The options are endless. You could choose a program in a country in Africa, Asia, Europe, South America, or anywhere else on the globe.

Travel broadens your perspective beyond the microcosm of college life. In today's world, it's important to see life from a wider view than the piece that you inhabit.

Every day the world is becoming smaller because of technological advances. Any international experience is useful, whether you use it in your career or hold on to the memories as a story to share with friends and family.

A bonus to studying abroad is how the experience will set you apart from the rest of the pack when applying for scholarships, internships, and jobs after graduation.

Do something out of the ordinary. Leave campus. Explore the local community. Travel the planet.

# 29

## TALK TO YOURSELF MORE THAN YOU LISTEN TO YOUSELF

**The mind is a powerful thing. Use it to your advantage.** What we focus our attention on with our thoughts – those worst-case scenarios that are often a figment of our imagination – sometimes end up coming true because of the energy we put into them.

Instead of listening to your fears and thinking about all those things you don't want to happen, try talking to yourself.

Tell yourself what you *would* like to happen. Visualize it happening. Write it down.

Talk to yourself more than you listen to yourself.

# 30

## TATTOOS ARE PERMANENT

**Think twice before doing something it's almost impossible undo.**
If you choose to get a tattoo in a visible area of your body like your neck or arms, know that many people – including potential employers – will have a bias against you. This could mean the difference between getting hired or ignored.

Keep in mind that if you choose to get a tattoo removed at a dermatologist's office with laser treatment, it can be expensive and painful.

Is it unfair to judge a book by the cover? Yes. Do people still do it? Yes.

It's your body and you can do with it what you choose. Just know that tattoos are permanent.

# 31

## THE MOST POWERFUL MEETING YOU CAN HAVE

**The most powerful meeting that you can have isn't a job interview. It's an informational meeting.**
An informational meeting is an opportunity to meet with someone you can learn from. It's a great way to expand your network, increase your influence, and build your brand.

The best way to secure an informational meeting is to tap into your existing network. Your network includes your family and friends, friends of friends, your professors, college alumni networks, social networks, people you've met at networking events, and beyond.

Once you identify people to contact, contact them with a brief email. Introduce yourself, share how you came across them, and tell them a little about yourself. From there, ask for 15 minutes of their time for an informational meeting to discuss what you would like to learn from them.

Once you secure the meeting, *prepare* as much as possible. Learn as much about the person, their background, and their work as you can. Review any information about them on the Internet. Prepare great questions and have a goal of what you'd like to get out of the meeting.

During the meeting, the focus should be on them. You're there to learn and to be a sponge. Soak up their wisdom. Most of the time, the meeting will shift to you. When it does, be ready to talk about your aspirations and goals and to share your story.

**Do not ask for a job during an informational meeting.** If you do ask for a job, you will immediately lose any goodwill or trust that you've built. Instead, be so impressive that they want to learn more.

### How to End the Meeting
First, always ask, *"Is there anyone else you think I should meet?"* If they're impressed by your preparation and questions, they'll gladly refer you to someone for another informational meeting.

Second, follow-up by sending a handwritten thank you card **(see #43)**.

# 32

## WHAT TO DO WHEN YOU DON'T KNOW WHAT TO DO

**Pick up the phone and call a friend.**
Go for a walk in nature.

Say a prayer.

Write in a journal.

Work out at the gym.

Read a motivational book.

When you don't know what to do, do something.

# 33

## JUST BECAUSE YOU'RE GOOD AT SOMETHING...

**...doesn't mean you're supposed to be doing it.**
This doesn't make sense, right? Or does it?

Over the course of your life, you're going to find things that you excel at. Sometimes, the things you happen to be exceptionally good at are things that you really don't enjoy doing.

This poses a dilemma – I'm good at this, but I don't like it. So what do you do?

Well, you can keep doing what you're good at and allow many years to pass you by along the way. Or, you can pivot, get curious, and pursue those things that truly interest you.

If you're lucky, you'll find what Gay Hendricks calls your "Zone of Genius" in his book, *The Big Leap*.

Always remember: Just because you're good at something, doesn't mean that you're supposed to be doing it.

# 34

## COLLABORATE

**Don't do it all by yourself.**
Together = better.

Bring out the best in others and allow them to bring out the best in you.

# 35

## TELL A STORY, NOT THE WHOLE STORY

**Attention spans are getting shorter and shorter. This is an unfortunate reality.**
Keep this in mind the next time you share a story with a group or person.

Your opportunity is to share those things that are essential – that make people lean in and want to learn more.

Have a beginning, middle, and end. Know where you're going with the story.

Tell a story, not the whole story.

# 36

## JOB INTERVIEWS: HAVE AN AGENDA

**If you go into a job interview *only* prepared to answer the questions that you're asked, you're not setting yourself up for success.**
Your job is to go into interviews prepared with an *agenda*.

Whether the interview lasts 5 minutes, 30 minutes, or an hour, besides answering their questions, make sure you find creative ways to share key things that the employer *must* know about you.

These include life experiences that make you unique.

Maybe you studied abroad, served in the military, are a student athlete, regularly contribute to a photography blog, work full-time job while attending school full-time, volunteer at an after-school program, or took a mission trip with your church.

Find those things that people must know about you – those things that don't always show up on a resume. Doing this will help you stand out from the crowd and distinguish yourself from the competition.

# 37

## FOUR QUESTIONS TO ASK WHEN THINGS GO BAD (OR GOOD*)

What happened?

Why did it happen?

What role did I play in it?

What can I/we do to ensure this *never* happens again?

What can I/we do to ensure this *does* happen again?*

# 38

## FIND GOOD FRICTION

**Friction can be a good thing.**
Imagine that you're lost in the woods and cold, but you have two sticks and some kindling. When you rub those sticks together, you create *friction* that can start a fire.

Now, imagine that you're in a car and it's stuck in the snow with the tires spinning. The car won't move. If you put some sand or salt underneath the tire, you can create some *friction* to help the car move forward.

Consider this: Diamonds are formed from carbon under millions and millions of years of pressure. Their beauty comes from friction.

On campus and in your life, seek out *good friction*.

Get feedback on your assignments. Know that the red ink on your essay serves to make it better. Spend time with allies because they're going to push your buttons and not accept your excuses. They'll make you better. Be willing to share your opinion even if it goes against what everyone else believes.

Good friction is where growth, development, and breakthroughs happen. There's always an opportunity to improve, develop, and stretch yourself.

# 39

## SAY IT BEFORE YOU RUN OUT OF BREATH

**People are always going to ask you some version of: *"What do you want to do after you graduate?"*** Always have an answer ready to go – with one rule: By the time you run out of breath, you should have completed your answer.

The easiest way to answer this question is by including the *position*, *industry*, and *type of company* you're looking to work with.

For example: *"I'm looking for an entry-level marketing position in the television industry with a company like Nickelodeon."*

If you're clear and concise, your reward will be hearing, *"Tell me more about that."*

# 40

## YOUR FAMILY & FRIENDS WON'T ALWAYS UNDERSTAND

**Sometimes what's best for you will make others uncomfortable.**
And that's ok.

People who've known us for most of our lives view us in a certain way. When we make decisions that they disagree with, or when we take the road less traveled, this can knock them off balance.

Most of the time, our family and friends want what's best for us. But what's best for *them* isn't always best for us.

Have an honest talk with people. Share why you're making the decision that you're making. Listen to their concerns and then, make the decision that's right for *you*.

At the end of the day, the decision is yours.

# 41

## "US" & "WE" IS GREATER THAN "I" & "ME"

**Be inclusive.**
Regularly audit your speaking and writing to see if you're making it solely about you.

It's all about the "us" and the "we." This is what brings us together.

"I" and "me" keeps us apart.

# 42

## AVOID THE PLACE YOU GO TO GIVE UP

**At some point, we find ourselves wanting to give up – to throw in the towel.**
It could be our education, a relationship, a business, or a project.

I was reminded of this during a trip to Nicaragua. One morning, as I walked around a sleepy surfing town, I stumbled into a café seeking Wi-Fi. Immediately upon entering the café, I knew something was off.

The interior of the bar was in dark contrast with the city. Outside it was sunny and bright. Inside it was dank and smoky. Though it wasn't even 9am, the bar was full of people drinking and chain-smoking. The faces at the bar looked tired, worn out and depressed.

People didn't come to this place to seek free Wi-Fi. They came to this place to give up. At least that's what my gut told me. I knew that the longer I stayed in this place, the worse I would feel. So, I left.

Right after stepping outside, it felt like a weight had been lifted off my shoulders. In an attempt to boost my spirits, I sought out another café, and I found one. *Just two doors down.*

This place was the exact opposite of the first. It was bright and airy. The walls and the music were colorful. The patrons wore smiles on their faces. Instead of alcohol in their mugs, there was fresh-squeezed juice or herbal tea.

My energy level immediately spiked. Who would've thought this place could be just two doors down?

During a rough patch, when it's easy to give up, we have to be careful where and how we spend our time and energy.

The good thing is that if we're patient and willing to "look around," we can find the perfect place that energizes us — where people support us to feel empowered.

Next time you find yourself ready to give up, pay close attention to your surroundings. What you need most could be just two doors down.

# 43

## WRITE HANDWRITTEN THANK YOU CARDS

**No, these aren't old-fashioned.**
When someone does something kind for you, don't just send and email and be instantly delete-able. Instead, write a handwritten card and mail it to them.

This shows that you took the time to purchase stationery, write a note by hand, and venture to the post office to mail it.

Handwritten thank you cards allow you to be memorable. They go a long way.

The time they take to write requires us to push pause on life to acknowledge someone else's kindness or generosity.

# 44

## BREAK THE CYCLE

**Routines can be great. They can keep us focused, on track, and in a rhythm.**
However, now and then, it's important to *break the cycle*.

Be willing to listen to music that's not your type of music.

Go to places that aren't the kind of places you'd normally go.

Eat what you normally wouldn't eat.

Mix it up. Break the cycle and see what you learn.

# 45

## YOUR FIRST "REAL JOB" WON'T BE YOUR LAST JOB

**Students regularly worry about making the wrong choice when it comes to their first job after college.** Good news: There's no right or wrong or wrong decision. Why? Because your first "real job" won't be your last job.

The job market and economy has changed. People no longer have lifelong employment. Actually, people now change jobs every two years on average.

So no need to stress yourself out wondering if you're selecting the "right job." Instead, get curious.

Ask yourself if there are great development opportunities in whatever job you select.

Ask yourself if the job is in a city that you're excited to explore.

Ask yourself if you'll be challenged.

Turn whatever fear you're feeling into excitement. And always remember: There is no wrong decision.

Your first "real job" won't be your last job.

# 46

## IT'S JUST WATER

**Once when I was in Juneau, Alaska, I noticed that something off.**
It was raining. But no one, *except me*, was using an umbrella. No one.

It didn't make any sense.

So, I walked up to a local to solve this mystery. The guy I approached was wearing glasses and they were covered with large droplets of water from the rain, as were his jacket, pants, and shoes.

"Sir, I'm from out of town," I said. "I noticed that none of the locals are using an umbrella. Why is this?"

After looking at me and my large umbrella he said, *"You know man, it's just water."*

I was floored. *It's just water!*

At once, everything made sense. Before I could say anything more, he walked away.

So when you're having a bad day, things aren't going your way, or you get caught in a real rainstorm, remember that it's just water.

In time, the water will always dry. And better yet, you'll have an opportunity to learn from it.

Researchers are finding that the true indicator of success is something called grit. Grit is your willingness to persevere – even through the toughest circumstances – to move closer and closer to your goal. This resilience through the "water" builds character and confidence.

Always remember when the going gets tough: It's just water.

# 47

## GIVE THANKS, THEN GIVE BACK

**At the end of each day, find a way to give thanks and acknowledge all that's good in your life.**
You can do this through prayer, writing in a gratitude journal, or meditating on all that's good.

Sure, everything may not be perfect. Maybe you had a rough day, week, or year. And…there's always something to be grateful for. This includes shelter, food, clothing, friendships, and so much more.

It's important to remind ourselves of this every day.

Then, if you have the means, give back. This doesn't require money. All it requires is your time. There's always someone who could use some support and guidance.

This could be a classmate, a fellow intern, someone you mentor, or a teammate.

Give back. Share what you've learned with others.

# 48

## THERE ARE NO METRICS FOR GRIT & RESILIENCE

**A piece of paper doesn't tell the whole story.**
When the New England Patriots defeated the Seattle Seahawks in the 2015 Super Bowl, there was something missing on the football field. Not a single starter in the Super Bowl was a "5-star athlete" coming out of high school.

5-star athletes are regarded as the best of the best. Yet, the most prestigious, high profile football game was being battled out by two star quarterbacks who weren't even close to being top draft picks.

This could be the case for you. Maybe you don't have great work experience on your resume, don't attend a top-ranked university, or don't have the most in-demand skills. You may not look good "on paper."

However, always remember: A piece of paper doesn't tell the full story. It can't measure grit and resilience. It can't measure *potential*.

Algorithms searching for key words won't find commitment, dedication, and hard work.

Stay creative, offer new perspectives, work hard, and don't give up.

If you're the diamond in the rough, you won't be for long.

# 49

## NO ONE CARES MORE THAN YOU

**No one cares more about your life and goals than you do.**
Yes, your parents care.

Yes, your friends care.

Yes, your significant other cares.

Yes, your professors care.

But, no one can, or should, care *more* than you.

# 50

## STAY CURIOUS

**Always stay curious.**
When you receive feedback and suggestions, even if it's tough to hear, stay curious.

Listen from an open perspective instead of a defensive point of view.

Even if you disagree, ask yourself, *"I wonder what I can learn from this?"*

Sometimes feedback or the red ink on an assignment can be a major learning opportunity for us to grow and develop.

# FINALLY, HAVE FUN

Because none of it matters unless you enjoy the ride.

# ACKNOWLEDGEMENTS

Thank you to all of the college students who inspire me.

Thank you to Katie Hendricks and The Hendricks Institute for teaching me how to take a conscious approach to life.

Thank you to Shiwani Srivastava for editing this book

Thank you to my wife for always having my back.

Thank you to all of my allies who make me better.

# ABOUT THE AUTHOR

**Antonio Neves is an internationally recognized speaker, writer, and author on leadership, communication, and the millennial workforce.** The go-to expert on helping young professionals achieve their potential, Antonio has delivered hundreds of keynotes to college students, recent graduates, and corporate and trade association audiences.

An award-winning journalist, Antonio worked in the television industry for 10 years as a correspondent, host, and producer with top networks including NBC, PBS, BET Networks, and Nickelodeon. Antonio's business articles regularly appear in Inc.com and Entrepreneur.com.

A former NCAA Division I student-athlete, Neves is the author of *Student Athlete 101: College Life Made Easy On & Off The Field*. A graduate of Western Michigan University and the Columbia University Graduate School of Journalism, Antonio lives in Los Angeles with his wife and two kids.

**To Learn More, Visit:**
www.TheAntonioNeves.com

**Join the Conversation on Facebook, Twitter and YouTube:**
@TheAntonioNeves

**For Booking:**
Tel: 888-559-7629
email: booking@theantonioneves.com

Made in the USA
Middletown, DE
27 June 2016